YOUNG SCIENTISTS INVESTIGATE

Electricity

Published by Evans Brothers Limited
2A Portman Mansions
Chiltern Street
London W1M 1LE

© copyright Evans Brothers Limited 1997

First published 1997
Reprinted 2000

British Library Cataloguing in Publication data.
A catalogue record for this book is available from the British Library.

Printed in Hong Kong by Wing King Tong

0 237 51688 8

Acknowledgements

Editorial: Su Swallow
Design: Neil Sayer
Production: Jenny Mulvanny
Commissioned photography: Alan Towse

The publishers would like to thank Mrs Gibson, the staff, parents and children of Booker Avenue Infant School for their help in the preparation of this book. We would also like to thank the children of Woolton Infant School who appear on the cover of this book.

For permission to reproduce copyright material the authors and publishers gratefully acknowledge the following:
Page 6 Chad Ehlers, Robert Harding Picture Library   page 8 Mike Agliolo, Robert Harding Picture Library   page 10 Chad Ehlers, Robert Harding Picture Library   page 20 David Hughes, Robert Harding Picture Library   page 24 Frankreich Burgund, Robert Harding Picture Library   page 26 Robert Harding Picture Library   page 28 Gordon Garradd, Science Photo Library

YOUNG SCIENTISTS INVESTIGATE

Electricity

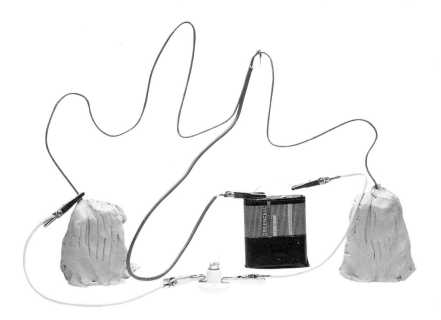

Malcolm Dixon
and Karen Smith

Evans

Evans Brothers Limited

NOTES FOR TEACHERS AND PARENTS

It's electric! (pages 6-7)
Use these pages to develop children's awareness of electricity as an important and convenient source of energy. Discuss what their lives would be like if we did not have this power source. Stress the dangers of mains electricity and the need to obey safety rules.

Electric lights (pages 8-9)
It may be possible to collect a variety of electric bulbs to show the children. Since they are made of glass careful supervision will be needed. The photograph shows a 4.5 volt battery (and 3.5 volt bulb) being used. This is useful because of the large terminals. 3 volt or 1.5 volt batteries (use 1.5 volt bulbs) could also be used. Sticky tape could be used to make firm connections. Match the bulb to the voltage of the battery as indicated above.
These batteries are a safe source of electricity to use with young children.

Warning lights (pages 10-11)
The circuit used in this model is similar to the basic circuit constructed in the *Electric lights* section. If possible obtain and use a 'flashing' bulb. Sweet containers and plastic bottles make suitable lighthouse shapes.

Switch on and off (pages 12-13)
Switching on an electrical device causes a gap to be closed and this causes electricity to flow around a circuit. Switching off causes the reverse to happen.

Making sounds (pages 14-15)
When making the model burglar alarm ensure all connections are tight especially between the bared wire ends and the kitchen foil. Buzzers can be purchased from electrical suppliers. Some buzzers have red and black wires – the red wire needs to be connected to the positive terminal of the battery. A bulb or bell could be used in place of a buzzer.

Good conductors (pages 16-17)
Insulators make it safe for us to use electricity. Remind children of the dangers of mains electricity. For the investigation include metal objects such as tin cans, aluminium foil, brass keys, scissors. Encourage the children to make predictions. The conductors will all be made of metal. The non-metal, graphite, used in pencil 'leads' is a conductor. The children's results could be recorded in tabular form.

Computers (pages 18-19)
When the crocodile clips are attached to a question and correct answer the circuit is completed and the bulb lights. An incorrect answer means that the circuit remains incomplete and the bulb does not light. Let the children make a variety of quiz cards.

Sending messages (pages 20-21)
Further discussion on the ways we use electricity could focus on messages received on the radio and, perhaps, through fax machines and computers. At school it may be possible to show a fax machine in use. The circuit should be set up as in the photograph. Ensure all connections are tight. When sending messages it may be more realistic if the sender is out of sight, in another room. Longer wires may well be needed.

Electric motors (pages 22-23)
Discuss the role of motors in making movement possible in machines. For this activity, a small motor powered by a 4.5 volt battery, obtainable from a model shop or school supplier, is suitable. When constructing the model adult use of a glue-gun will be helpful. Care should be taken with the rotating plastic propeller.

Using conductors (pages 24-25)
A device called a pantograph carries the electricity from the overhead wires to the train. 'Dodgem' fairground cars also pick up electricity from above them. The photograph shows a completed circuit. Coat hanger wire is suitable for the zig-zag shape. It may need to be rubbed with glass-paper to remove any protective lacquer.

Where Does It Come From? (pages 26-27)
Power stations can be coal, oil, water, wind, gas, solar or nuclear powered. If possible visit a local power station. To save electrical energy children may suggest that lights are switched off when not needed and that electrical heating systems are turned down. Reminders about the dangers of mains electricity are appropriate.

Static electricity (pages 28-29)
'Current' electricity flows along wires. 'Static' electricity does not move. Rubbing produces a 'charge' which attracts or repels. The balloons become negatively charged and repel each other. The comb becomes negatively charged and attracts hair and water. Make sure the hair is dry for this investigation and that the comb does not touch the water.

Contents

It's electric!   6

Electric lights   8

Warning lights   10

Switch on and off   12

Making sounds   14

Good conductors   16

Computers   18

Sending messages   20

Electric motors   22

Using conductors   24

Where does it come from?   26

Static electricity   28

Index   30

The activities in this book are probably best supervised by an adult. They should be used to stress the dangers of mains electricity and the importance of following safety rules.

It's electric!

We use electricity in many different ways. Most people light their homes using electricity. It is used to power cookers, heaters, televisions, refrigerators, washing machines, computers and many other things that we use in our homes. People use things that work by electricity when they are at work, too.

Electricity is an important part of our lives. Can you imagine what life would be like without electricity?

 ## Work with a friend

Talk about the ways you use electricity in your home.
Make drawings of the things that use electricity in your home, or make a display of things that use electricity.

⚠️ **MAINS ELECTRICITY CAN KILL.**
NEVER play with electric power points, plugs, switches, light sockets or machines.

Make sure you think about:

Which things use electricity to give light?
Which things use electricity to make sounds?
Which things use electricity to give heat?
Which things use electricity to make movement?

Electric lights

Electric light bulbs are used to light up our homes, schools, streets, shops and factories. Inside these bulbs there is a short, coiled wire called a filament. When electricity goes through the filament it becomes hot and gives off light.

Ask an adult to show you the filament inside a household bulb. Use a magnifier to look at a small torch bulb. Can you see the filament?

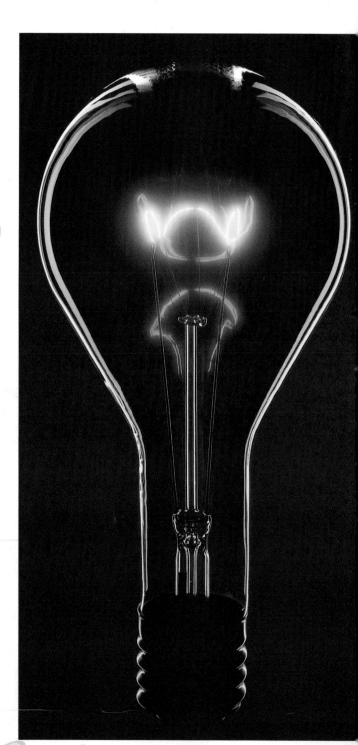

Make a bulb light up

Screw the bulb into the bulb holder. Use the screwdriver to fix the ends of the wires to the crocodile clips. Connect the crocodile clips to the bulb holder and battery so that the bulb lights up.

Electricity is flowing from the battery through the wires and bulb back to the battery.
This is called an 'electric circuit'.
Which part of the bulb is lit up?

You will need:
battery
bulb
bulb holder
pieces of wire
  with bared
  ends
4 crocodile
  clips
screwdriver

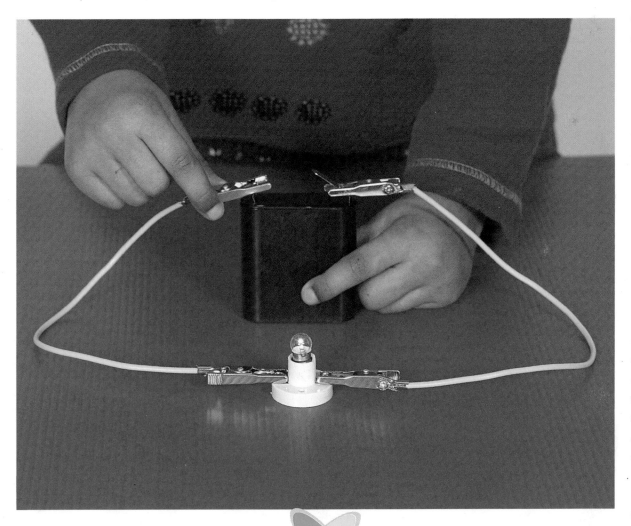

Warning lights

Some electric lights warn us of danger. Traffic lights tell drivers when to stop and when to go. Car drivers use lights to tell others when they are turning to the right or left. Look at the photograph. The flashing light on this lighthouse is warning ships about dangerous rocks. Can you think of other ways in which electric lights warn of danger?

Make a model lighthouse

Screw the bulb into the bulb holder. Connect the two wires to the bulb holder. Push the wires inside the container. Ask an adult to make a small hole in the side of the container. Pull the wires through this hole. Use crocodile clips to connect the wires to the battery. Check that the bulb lights up. Glue the bottle to the board. Glue the clear plastic pot to the bottle. Wrap card round the bottle and glue in place. Make 'rocks' from paper or use large stones. Place them around your lighthouse. Paint your model.

How can you make the light flash on and off?

You will need:

bulb
bulb holder
battery
2 crocodile clips
2 lengths of wire
  with bared ends
small wooden
  board
plastic bottle
strong glue
clear plastic pot
card
paper
paints
scissors

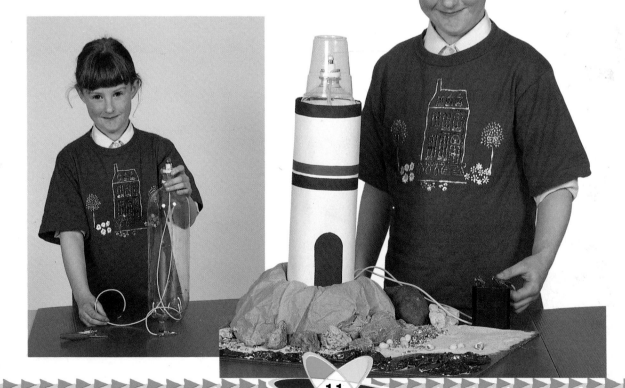

Switch on and off

It is easy to switch electricity 'on' when we need it and 'off' when we do not.
A switch makes a gap in an electric circuit. When the switch is 'off' electricity cannot flow across the gap. When the switch is 'on' the gap is closed and so electricity can flow.

What happens when you switch on the lights in a room?
What happens when you switch off a television?
Do you have a special safety switch in your bathroom?
Can you think of more kinds of switches in your home?

Make a switch

Screw the bulb into the bulb holder. To make a switch, first fold some card in half. Press two paper fasteners through one side of the card, fixing a rectangle of folded kitchen foil to one of the fasteners. Use the wires and crocodile clips to make a circuit. Connect a wire to each of the paper fasteners.

Now move the foil to close the gap between the paper fasteners. Your switch is 'on'. What happens?

Why does this happen?
Switch 'off'. What happens? Why?

You will need:

card
paper fasteners
kitchen foil
battery
bulb
bulb holder
3 lengths of wire
    with bared ends
4 crocodile clips
screwdriver

Making sounds

Sounds come from televisions, radios, telephones
and doorbells. These sounds are made using
electricity.
Some buildings have burglar alarms. They make a
loud noise using electricity. One kind of alarm is
placed under carpets. If a thief treads on it, the
alarm makes a very loud noise.

Have you seen a burglar alarm on the side of a
building? Have you ever heard the sound of a
burglar alarm?

Make a burglar alarm

Fold the card in half. Glue foil inside each half. Cut a small piece of foam and glue it to the card as shown in the photograph. Staple the bared end of a wire to the foil on one side of the card. Do the same with another wire to the other piece of foil. Connect these wires, in a circuit, with a small buzzer and battery. Press the two sides of the card together so that the foil pieces touch. Does the buzzer sound?

You will need:

card
kitchen foil
thin foam
glue
battery
small buzzer
4 crocodile clips
3 lengths of wire
   with bared ends
stapler

Place your alarm so that it warns you of visitors coming into a room.

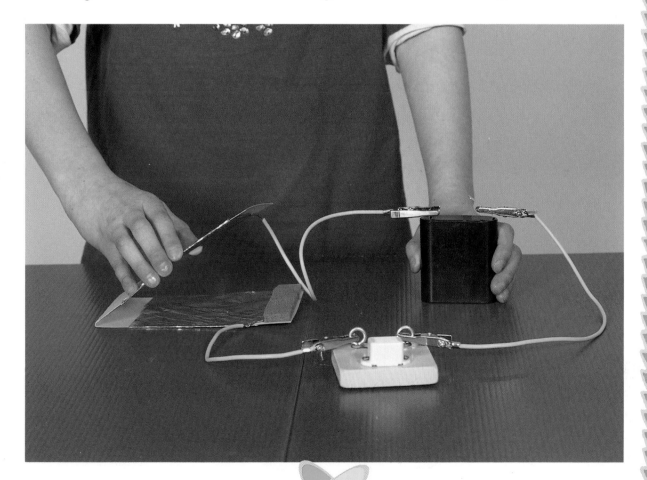

Good conductors

Electricity flows easily through some materials. These materials are called conductors. Metals are good conductors.
A material that electricity does not flow through is called an insulator. Plastic, rubber and wood are insulators.

Look at the photograph. The wires are made of a metal called copper. Copper is a good conductor and so electricity flows easily through it. The wires are covered in plastic. Electricity does not flow through plastic.

What would happen if the wires were not covered by plastic?

Testing conductors

You can test to see which things are good conductors. Which materials do you think electricity will flow through? Use this circuit to see if you are right.

Connect each object, in turn, to the crocodile clips. When the bulb lights up you are testing a conductor. It lets the electricity flow around the circuit. Electricity does not flow through insulators and the bulb will not light up. What do you notice about the materials that are conductors of electricity?

You will need:
battery
bulb
bulb holder
2 crocodile clips
3 lengths of wire with
  bared ends
screwdriver
a collection of
  objects made from
  rubber, cork, plastic,
  wood, cardboard,
  fabric and metals

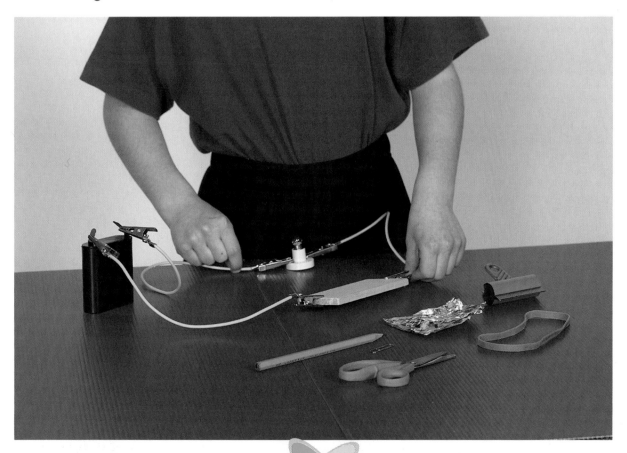

Computers

Many children have computers in their classrooms. Some children have a computer at home. You can use a computer to write a story and print it out on a printer. You can use a computer to help you with sums and find out facts. Have you ever played a game on a computer?

Computers work because of electricity. They contain special electric circuits.

Make an electric quiz game

Make a quiz card. The answers should be mixed up (look at the photograph below). Use 5 lengths of wire and paperclips to connect each question to the correct answer. The wires should run along the back of the quiz card.

Connect the battery and bulb, using the wires and crocodile clips. What happens when you fix one crocodile clip to a question and the other crocodile clip to the correct answer? Now try a wrong answer. What happens?

Make other cards like this to test your friends.

You will need:
battery
bulb in a
  bulbholder
8 lengths of wire
  with bared ends
10 paperclips
card
  6 crocodile clips.

7 + 2	20
6 − 5	6
3 × 6	9
12 ÷ 2	18
10 × 2	1

Sending messages

Electricity helps us to send messages over great distances. You can use a telephone to speak to your friends and to someone in another country. When you watch television you can see and hear things that are happening far away from your home. Many people use computers to send messages to each other. Can you think of other messages you get at home because of electricity?

Sending messages without words

Connect the wires to the bulbs, drawing pins and battery.

Press a paperclip switch. Which bulb lights up ?
What happens when you press the other switch?

Can you think of a way to send a message to a friend? Could you use a code?

You will need:
battery
2 bulbs
2 bulb holders
4 long lengths of wire with bared ends
2 short lengths of wire with bared ends
4 drawing pins
2 paperclips
2 pieces of wood
screwdriver

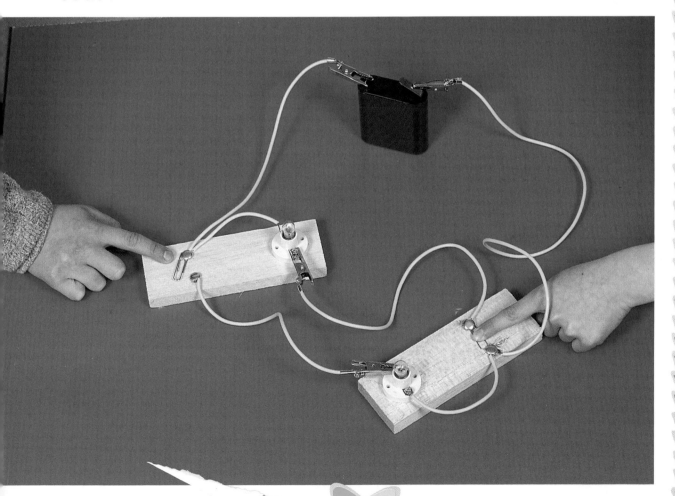

Electric motors

At home we use machines such as hairdryers, vacuum cleaners, food mixers and washing machines. All these things use electric motors. The motors use electricity and make things turn.
Do any of your toys have electric motors inside them?

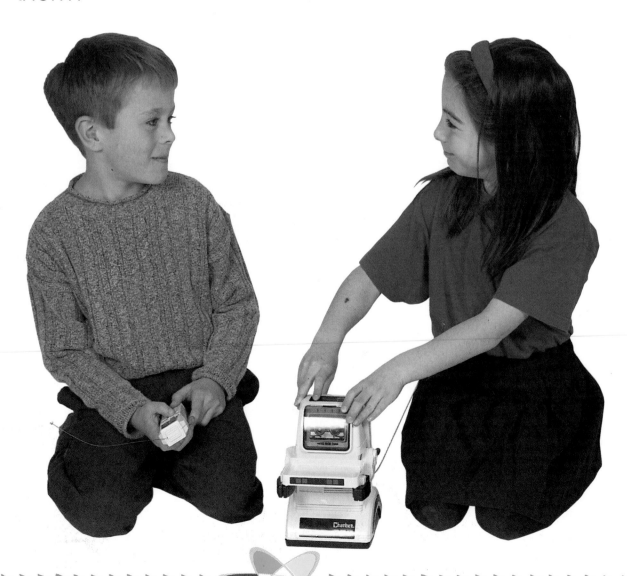

Make a model motorboat

You will need:

Ask an adult to help you.

Fix the propeller to the motor. It should be a tight fit.

Use sticky tape to fix the motor to the bottom of the yoghurt pot.

Glue the yoghurt pot to the piece of wood.

Attach the wood to two plastic bottles with elastic bands. Use crocodile clips to connect the motor to a battery.

Test your model to see if it moves on water.

small electric
  motor
small plastic
  propeller
battery
2 crocodile clips
2 plastic bottles
piece of balsa
  wood
yoghurt pot
elastic bands
sticky tape
strong glue
screwdriver

Using conductors

We use trains, cars, buses and aeroplanes to move from place to place. All of these use electricity in some way.

Some of the fastest trains in the world get their power from wires that run above them. Look at the photograph. How does the electricity get from the overhead wire to the train? The electricity turns motors, inside the train, and these move the wheels.

Turn a conductor into a game

Bend the stiff wire into a zig-zag shape. Push each end into some plasticine. Use the crocodile clips and covered wires to connect the stiff wire to the bulb and battery. Connect another wire to the battery. Bend one end of this wire into a loop around the zig-zag wire.

Try to move the loop along the zig-zag wire without them touching. What happens when the loop touches the zig-zag wire? Why does this happen?

You will need:
plasticine
stiff and bare wire
battery
3 lengths of wire
  with bared ends
5 crocodile clips
bulb
bulb holder,
screwdriver

Where does it come from?

Electricity is made in power stations. Wires carry the electricity from the power station to your home, into schools, shops, hospitals, cinemas and factories. Sometimes these wires hang from tall pylons. In towns and cities the electricity flows through wires buried below the ground.

Electricity comes into your home and school through wires. We call this mains electricity. The electricity flows through wires, hidden inside the walls and under floors and ceilings, to the lights and power points.

Ask an adult to show you the electricity meter inside your home or school. You can see the wire that brings electricity to the building. The meter shows how much electricity is being used so that it can be paid for. Electricity is expensive. Can you think of ways to save using electricity?

⚠ **REMEMBER – MAINS ELECTRICITY CAN KILL.**

Static electricity

The electricity that we use from the mains and batteries is called 'current electricity'. Another kind of electricity is called 'static electricity'. The lightning that we see flashing in the sky, in a storm, is caused by static electricity.

Static electricity is made when two things rub together. Have you ever heard crackling sounds when you are undressing or combing your hair?

Investigate static electricity!

Rub two balloons with wool and bring them near to each other.
What happens?

Rub a plastic comb with wool.
Hold the comb near your hair.
What happens?

Rub the comb with wool again.
Hold it near a fine stream of water from a tap.
Move the comb around.
What do you notice?

Index

A

aeroplanes 24

B

burglar alarms 14
buses 24

C

cars 24
circuits 12, 18
computers 6, 8, 20
conductors 16
cookers 6
current electricity
 28

D

doorbells 14

F

filament 8
food mixers 22

H

hairdryers 22
heaters 6

L

light bulbs 8
lighthouse 10
lightning 28

M

motors 22, 24

P

power stations 26
pylons 26

R

radios 14
refrigerators 6

S

static electricity 28
switches 12

T

telephones 14, 20
televisions 6, 12,
 14, 20
toys 22
traffic lights 10
trains 24

V

vacuum cleaners
 22

W

washing machines
 6, 22
work 6